LONDON NIGHT BUSES SINCE 1984

PHILIP WALLIS

AMBERLEY

First published 2021

Amberley Publishing
The Hill, Stroud
Gloucestershire, GL5 4EP

www.amberley-books.com

ISBN 978 1 3981 0044 2 (print)
ISBN 978 1 3981 0045 9 (ebook)

British Library Cataloguing in Publication Data.
A catalogue record for this book is available from the British Library.

Orgination by Amberley Publishing.
Printed in the UK.

Contents

Acknowledgements

I am most grateful to photographers Paul Davis, Malc McDonald and Roy Waterhouse for allowing me access to their Night Bus photographic collections and for permission to publish images. Their contributions have combined with my own pictures to allow a representative pictorial display of Night Bus operations.

The London Omnibus Traction Society (LOTS) kindly granted permission to extract information from its extensive range of publications. I have drawn upon research from my two-volume work *London's Night Buses*, published by Capital Transport in 2011 and 2013.

Development of Night Bus Network 1984–2020

Note on the Text

Night Bus routes often operate either side of midnight over two successive days, with service starting in the late evening of one day and finishing in the early morning hours of the next day. Dates quoted generally reflect this, for example: 13/14 April 1984.

This book covers the period 13/14 April 1984 to 30/31 December 2020.

Peak Vehicle Requirement (PVR) Night Bus Routes 13/14 April 1984–30/31 December 2019

Date	Sunday – Thursday nights (Su–Th)	Friday – Saturday nights (Fr–Sa)
12/13 April 1984 (Final night of traditional network)	59	61
13/14 April 1984 (First night of expanded network)	77	78
1/2 November 1985	86	109
20/21 November 1987	96	130
9/10 February 1990	128	167
17/18 July 1992	137	177
11/12 March 1994	155	191
28/29 November 1997	209	284
7/8 January 2000	257	352
1/2 July 2000 (Final night of LRT control)	261	356
30 November/1 December 2001	375	503
12/13 December 2003	509	642
16/17 December 2005	531	685
28/29 December 2007	592	772
27/28 November 2009	622	830
30/31 December 2011	633	875
27/28 July – 12/13 August 2012 (Enhanced service for Olympic Games)	735	939
30/31 December 2013	635	892
30/31 December 2015	660	974
11/12 February 2017 (Highest PVR)	682	1,049
30/31 December 2017	659	941
30/31 December 2018	630	841
30/31 December 2019	624	831
20/21 March 2020 (First lockdown: Su–Th schedules on all nights)	619	619

By 28/29 August 2020 (Fr–Sa schedules restored except weekend Night Tube-connected routes)	617	775
30/31 December 2020	617	775

London's Night Bus network provides nightly bus services over 117 routes. Bus allocations to work the network increased exponentially between 1984 and early 2017. The introduction of weekend Night Tube services in 2016 caused lower demand for some Night Bus routes which, combined with Transport for London's (TfL) efficiency drive to tackle its operating deficit, reduced bus allocations between 2017 and 2019. The start of the coronavirus pandemic in March 2020 saw Sunday to Thursday night schedules applied on all nights of the week. Friday and Saturday night schedules had been restored to most routes by 28/29 August 2020.'

Traditional Network

London's traditional Night Bus network had remained largely unchanged for decades. Its few routes, some with tramway origins, were primarily intended to serve night workers in the newspaper industry around Fleet Street and early morning workers, such as in London's commodity markets and post offices. Schedules were often irregular with no Saturday night/Sunday morning service over most routes.

Accusations of inefficiency and waste within London Transport (LT) led to reviews of that executive's functions, including the Night Bus operation. Consultants from Oxford University were commissioned in 1980 to appraise the network and presented their review to LT in October 1981. Key recommendations of the Oxford Report were as follows:

1. The existing Night Bus network be scrapped and replaced by a core network of nine cross-London routes terminating 5 miles beyond Trafalgar Square. Passengers travelling further out would be expected to use demand responsive taxis.
2. Saturday night/Sunday morning operation be extended to more routes.
3. Clock face (regular interval) headways to be adopted.
4. Increased use of one-person-operated buses.

London Transport did not accept all the recommendations of the Oxford Report, particularly rejecting the concept of demand responsive taxis. Instead, LT chose to modify its existing network to meet present and latent demand. Saturday night/Sunday morning operation was extended across the entire Night Bus network from 29/30 October 1983. LT's plan to launch an extended route network in February 1984 was frustrated by trade union opposition to increased single manning. Agreement between the parties was eventually secured which allowed an expanded network to be introduced on 13/14 April 1984.

Major Expansion from 13/14 April 1984

The number of Night Bus routes increased from twenty-six to thirty-seven from Friday night/Saturday morning of 13/14 April 1984. New areas served by the network included Bromley, Edgware, Harold Hill, Richmond and Uxbridge. Most routes operated hourly clock face headways. All routes bar N29 (Enfield), N93 (Hampstead Heath) and

Inter-Station were one-person-operated. Trafalgar Square became the focal point for all central London routes. The majority of routes were operated by T-type Leyland Titans or M-type MCW Metrobuses although DM/DMS-type Daimler/Leyland Fleetlines were allocated to five routes and the N96 (Chingford Station) remained the sole single-deck route with LS-type Leyland Nationals. Unexpectedly, the N93 (previously Fleetline-operated) gained a Routemaster allocation.

London Regional Transport Control

London Regional Transport (LRT) assumed powers from 29 June 1984. LRT set up subsidiary London Buses Ltd (LBL) to take control of six bus operating districts.

Demand for the expanded Night Bus network quickly soared. Unscheduled duplicates were added to many routes on weekend nights and incorporated into timetables during 1985. Weekend nights' bus allocations became broadly 35 per cent higher than on weeknights.

The predictability of regular clock face headways was an important factor in attracting and retaining passengers. LRT did not wish to jeopardise network reliability due to lost journeys, so from 26/27 October 1984, it arranged for an Emergency Stand-By bus to be available to substitute for missing buses on any central London-serving Night Bus route. The number of Stand-By buses increased to three as the network grew. This expansion, accelerated to a large extent by relaxed licensing laws and development of the night-time economy, ultimately resulted in operators becoming contractually responsible for the entire operation of their services and the Emergency Stand-By buses were stood down in May 2002.

Complete one-person operation of the Night Bus network was achieved from 22/23 April 1985 – over twenty years before this was achieved across London's daytime bus route network.

Service frequencies started to increase from 1985 with 30-minute headways introduced on some routes, particularly at weekends, followed by the first 15-minute frequencies from 1986.

The first use of Leyland Olympians was on route N77 (Thamesmead) in 1987. Single-deck buses disappeared from the network that same year with the conversion of the N96 to double-deck Leyland Titans. Fleetlines enjoyed resurgence on Night Bus work with their allocation to Sutton garage-operated routes N68 and N88 in 1987.

Network Density Increases

Ten further Night Bus routes were introduced on 27/28 October 1989 and others were recast. Density of the network increased whilst new districts reached included Orpington, Isle of Dogs and Surbiton.

New routes N1 (Barnet) and N5 (Edgware) were identified in publicity and on bus blinds as 'Northern Line' to promote their night-time service when those two branches of that parallel Underground line were closed. Similarly, route N21 was branded as 'Piccadilly Line' when it was rerouted to run parallel to that Underground line to Cockfosters Station from 17/18 July 1992.

Single-deck buses returned to the network with the introduction of innovatory radial route N31 (Camden Town–Fulham Broadway) on 11/12 November 1989, operated by MA-type Mercedes-Benz midibuses.

Cross-London route N6 (Willesden–Walthamstow Central) was one of ten new Night Bus routes introduced on 27/28 October 1989. London Forest's Leyland Titan T 553 was loading outside the National Gallery in Trafalgar Square on that route's inaugural night of operation. (Roy Waterhouse)

Competition Develops

London Buses formed twelve wholly owned subsidiary companies on 1 April 1989 which introduced an element of competition between them. Competition intensified from 1 April 1993 when the block grant system was replaced by individual route tenders. Independent operators London Coaches gained Willesden routes N52/daytime 52 from 3/4 December 1993 and London Suburban Bus ran Kensal Rise routes N6/daytime 6 from 28/29 January 1994.

London Buses' subsidiary companies were privatised between January 1994 and January 1995. Serious competition for route contracts had arrived.

Leyland Fleetline usage on Night Bus work ended in 1991 with the conversion of routes N68, N87 and N88 to Metrobus operation. Scania N113s were operated for several years from 1992 by East London and London Northern. London Central used DAF DB250/Optare Spectras between 1993 and 1997. Large numbers of Volvo Olympians joined fleets between 1995 and 1997.

Autumn 1993/spring 1994 saw a further surge of new Night Bus route introductions. Amongst these, the N253 was the first regular three-number N route and gave useful radial links across north-east London.

Demand for Night Bus travel had increased such that by 24/25 November 1995, twenty-one routes had nightly 30-minute (or greater) frequencies over all, or sections of, their routes whilst another nine routes had their frequencies increased to 30 minutes on

Friday and Saturday nights. Seventeen routes operated hourly on a nightly basis. Route N155 operated every 10 minutes on Friday and Saturday nights over its section of route between Trafalgar Square and Tooting Broadway. The Aldwych to Streatham section of route N109 ran every 15 minutes nightly, as did sections of certain other routes on Friday and Saturday nights.

Route Numbering – London Regional Transport

London Transport had adopted a numerically descending Night Bus route number sequence from N99 on 11/12 October 1960. The network's expansion from 13/14 April 1984 partially continued that downward route number sequence with new routes N79 to N74 (although N75 was omitted) and partially introduced route numbers which bore numerical affinity to daytime services over common sections of route, viz. N2, N11, N13, N14, N18 and N27. Pre-existing route numbers N29 and N68 continued and new route N21 aligned with daytime route 221. Both sequences were subsequently extended through further route introductions, although certain new numbers did not fit any identifiable pattern, such as N50, N51 and N56 which replaced the Inter-Station Route from 26/27 April 1985. N66 was the lowest route number reached in the numerically descending sequence from N99 when introduced on 30/31 October 1993.

LRT had started to dismantle the LT-originated numerically descending route number sequence on 18/19 January 1991 when historically significant route N94 (Liverpool Street–Cricklewood), which had originated as the London General Omnibus Company's first all-night bus route 94 in 1913, was renumbered N16 to align it with the daytime 16 over common routeing between Cricklewood and Marble Arch. The big push came in summer 1995 when LRT publicity advised eleven routes would be renumbered to 'make the service even easier'. Night Bus routes, where possible, have been based on the corresponding daytime routes, using the same numbers prefixed by an 'N'. In all, twenty-four Night Bus routes were renumbered, the last being N81 to N89 (Trafalgar Square–Erith) on 28/29 June 2002. Route N97 (Trafalgar Square–Hammersmith Broadway) remained sole survivor of the numerically descending route numbers.

The continued use of Trafalgar Square as the focal point for all central London-serving Night Bus routes became impractical as the network and service frequencies increased. Between 1996 and 2000 eighteen services were routed away from the Square. This increased the importance of Night Bus hubs such as Oxford Circus and Tottenham Court Road Station.

London General-operated N37 became an element of LRT's first 24-hour service when introduced from 26/27 April 1997. The N37 and daytime 37 gave a seamless service between Peckham and Putney Station.

Early Low-floor Buses

The distinction of introducing low-floor bus operation to London's Night Bus network rests with First Centrewest when Camden Town to Fulham single-deck route N31 was converted from step-floor Dennis Dart to DM-type low-floor Marshall-bodied Dennis Dart SLF operation on 1/2 May 1998.

Low-floor double-deck operation on the Night Bus network was initiated by Stagecoach East London when Dennis Tridents replaced Leyland Titans as Barking garage's allocation to route N15 (Marble Arch–Romford Market) from 12/13 April 1999. First Capital became the second operator of low-floor double-deckers on Night Bus service with the introduction of Dennis Tridents upon its securing the contracts for routes N1 (Trafalgar Square–Plumstead) and N25 (Trafalgar Square–Barkingside or Harold Hill) from 25/26 June 1999 – in both instances step-floor buses were intermixed for a short while. First Centrewest's allocations to routes N18 (Trafalgar Square–Harrow Weald), N23 (Liverpool Street Station–Northolt) and N139 (Trafalgar Square–West Hampstead) were progressively converted to low-floor TN-type Dennis Tridents in July 1999. Metroline London Northern converted route N43 (Trafalgar Square–Friern Barnet) to TP-type Dennis Trident operation from 23/24 July 1999. Arriva London North was the fifth operator to put low-floor double-deckers into Night Bus service, with the official conversion of route N279 (Victoria Station–Waltham Cross) to DAF DB250LF DLA/DLP-type operation from 15/16 October 1999.

The first Volvo B7TL low-floor double-deckers were noted in Night Bus service on 31 January/1 February 2000 with London Central on route N159. Similar conversions followed quickly on routes N12, N36 and N84. This marked the end of Leyland Titan usage on Night Bus service apart from three at Camberwell garage retained for Emergency Stand-By duties (also used in daytime service) until May 2002.

Increasingly new Night Bus routes (and contract renewals) were specified for operation by low-floor buses such as Metroline-operated N140 (Harrow Weald–Heathrow Airport), LRT's final Night Bus route introduction on 31 March/1 April 2000, using Dennis Tridents.

Near-demise of LRT Routes beyond Greater London

London Regional Transport inherited two 'out-county' routes into Hertfordshire from London Transport, in the form of Potters Bar N80 and Hammond Street N90. LRT went on to develop further Night Bus services into neighbouring counties Essex, Hertfordshire, Kent and Surrey.

Such services started to decline from 28/29 January 1994 when the N18's service to Watford Junction (Hertfordshire) was cut back to Harrow Weald. Further cutbacks to services into Essex, Hertfordshire and Surrey followed until, following withdrawal of Potters Bar N91 journeys after 30/31 January 1997, only the N81's service into Kent and the N279's to Waltham Cross and Upshire remained. The Kent element of the N81, to Dartford, Gravesend and the Medway Towns, had become restricted to operation on Friday and Saturday nights only since 28/29 July 1995 when its weeknight service was curtailed at Crayford. LRT-sponsored night operation into Kent ended after 22/23 July 1999 when the N81 was cut back to terminate at Bexleyheath. The N279's nightly service to Waltham Cross (Hertfordshire), with one nightly return journey to Upshire (Essex), remained the sole LRT-sponsored Night Bus route to run beyond Greater London. Its Upshire journey last ran on 14/15 October 1999 but its service to Waltham Cross continues, giving the N279 unique status as the only contemporary Night Bus route to terminate outside London.

London Central introduced commercially operated routes N80 and N82 from central London to Gravesend and Gillingham from 23/24 July 1999. Operation was linked with pre-existing commercial route N60 to form a through cross-London service between Watford, Gravesend and Gillingham on weekend nights with an allocation of four buses. London Central's commercial Night Bus operation reduced from 12/13 May 2000 and was withdrawn after 18/19 May 2002.

New Year's Eve

Celebration of New Year's Eve increased massively after New Year's Day was made a bank holiday for the first time in 1974. For safety reasons, the authorities decided to close Trafalgar Square to vehicular traffic until the early hours from New Year's Eve 1976 onwards. Night Bus routes were curtailed or rerouted away from the Square's vicinity to hubs such as Aldwych, Cambridge Circus and Victoria Embankment, with extra bus allocations on most routes. Following the network's expansion from 13/14 April 1984, Aldwych became the principal focal point for Night Bus services on New Year's Eves.

The scale of celebrations grew so great that three Special Services were introduced on New Year's Eve 1989 to move crowds from the festivities to peripheral Night Bus termini and railway stations. Special New Year's Eve services ran over successive years until 2004, with varied routeings over that period. The need for special central London New Year's Eve services was negated by the introduction of overnight Underground services from New Year's Eve 2005. However, the threat of industrial action causing disruption to the Tube on New Year's Eve 2006 led to a hastily arranged Special Service.

Transport for London Control

The London Assembly was formed in 2000 along with the new office of Mayor of London, empowered with wide-ranging authority over the administration of Greater London. Transport policy has been overseen by Transport for London since 3 July 2000 with bus service operation controlled by London Bus Services Ltd (LBSL).

The vicinity of Tottenham Court Road Station is an important hub for Night Bus routes. Arriva London North's DAF DB250LF DLP 78 was seen on 11 June 2006 working route N279 to Waltham Cross in Hertfordshire. (Philip Wallis)

Ken Livingstone was the first elected mayor who wasted no time in issuing his Draft Transport Strategy, which included a commitment to introduce 'more off-peak and night services'. The biggest-ever increase in Night Bus routes followed with the introduction of forty-two new night-time routes, giving ninety-eight Night Bus routes at 30/31 August 2003 compared with fifty-six such routes just three years earlier. Route innovation then proceeded at a steady, but slower, pace with twenty-three new Night Bus routes (net of renumberings) being introduced between 2004 and 2010. Many of these formed the night-time element of 24-hour services covering all, or part, of daytime bus routes. Since then new route introductions have been few apart from a burst of activity between September 2015 and December 2016, related to the introduction of Night Tubes, when nineteen existing daytime routes gained night-time services, in all but two instances on weekend nights only.

LBSL quickly adopted a minimum frequency of 30 minutes nightly for Night Bus services – some routes have higher frequencies, particularly central London-serving ones at weekends.

Bifurcation of Night Bus routes was once quite common with services dividing to reach two different termini, usually at outer end. The last such routes, N8 (Victoria Station–Newbury Park Station or Woodford Wells) and N25 (Oxford Circus–Hainault or Harold Hill), operated on 24/25 June 2004.

Vehicle Policy – Transport for London

LBSL specified low-floor buses for its route contracts from the outset, although a few early contracts allowed initial step-floor bus operation. By 28/29 April 2001 thirty-seven Night Bus routes were worked by low-floor buses whilst a further thirteen routes shared step- and low-floor bus operation. M-type Metrobus usage on the Night Bus network ended in October 2001 when allocations on Metroline-operated routes N16 and N98 were converted to low-floor Dennis Tridents or Volvo B7TLs.

Casual substitution of step-floor buses on LBSL routes contracted for low-floor bus operation became precluded from 24 July 2004 by an edict which threatened operators with non-payment for any journeys so worked. TfL's ambition to achieve complete low-floor bus operation across its entire network by the end of 2005 sealed the fate of remaining step-floor buses, by then confined to Volvo Olympians. Route N381 (Whitehall–Peckham) was the last Night Bus route to have retained a step-floor bus allocation until 7/8 October 2004.

When TfL had assumed control just three routes – N28, N31 and N72 – were operated by single-deck buses. The number of single-deck-operated routes increased to ten following route introductions between 1/2 September 2000 and 31 January/1 September 2003, with the ubiquitous Dennis Dart SLF dominating allocations. Certain routes were subsequently converted to double-deck operation.

Mercedes-Benz Citaro articulated low-floor single-deckers (bendy buses) first entered Night Bus service on 14/15 March 2003 over Stagecoach Selkent-operated route N453. Night-time operation of bendy buses was extended to include 24-hour routes 12, 25 and 149 whilst the N29 became the fifth bendy bus-operated Night Bus route from 13/14 January 2006.

The Mayor of London's influence over transport policy was demonstrated following the election of Boris Johnson in May 2008. His mandate included a pledge to rid London of bendy buses, which he considered constituted a traffic hazard. All bendy bus-operated

Night Bus routes were converted to double-deck operation, starting with route 149 on 15/16 October 2010 and ending with the N29 on 25/26 November 2011.

Single-deck Night Bus routes reached their highest number at twelve with the introduction of a night-time service over route 33 from 29/30 January 2010. Numbers subsequently plummeted due to conversion of bendy bus routes, route withdrawals and double-decking of the 285 to leave four Night Bus routes operated by single-deck buses at 30/31 December 2020. These comprise routes N33, N72 and the night-time elements of 24-hour services 108 and 214.

Hybrid (electric battery pack/diesel engine) buses were first noted on Night Bus service in March 2010 when Metroline sometimes used AD Trident Enviro400Hs on route 139's night service. The night-time element of London United-operated 94 was the first Night Bus route to gain a formal allocation of hybrid buses, from 4/5 November 2010, with Enviro 400Hs. Use of hybrid buses increased progressively and was quickened by Mayor Sadiq Khan's 2017 policy introducing Low Emission Bus Zones across London and the Ultra-Low Emission Zone in April 2019. Diesel engine buses are in rapid decline across London and, at 30/31 December 2020, are confined to certain outer London routes.

Mayor Boris Johnson's competition to design a 'New Bus for London' was the genesis of the hybrid LT-type. Belatedly rebranded 'New Routemaster', these Wrightbus-built vehicles first entered Night Bus service with conversion of Metroline-operated 24-hour route 24 (Pimlico–Hampstead Heath) to LTs from 22/23 June 2013. The LT-type is now prolific on Night Bus service, mainly on routes serving central London and/or the City.

Metroline's LT 97 was photographed in Parliament Street working the night-time element of 24-hour service route 24. (Philip Wallis)

Battery-electric buses are gaining prominence across TfL's network. The first Night Bus route to be so operated was the night-time element of 24-hour route 214 when it was converted to operation by single-deck SEe-type BYD – AD Enviro200EVs in August 2019. Metroline and London United began operation of double-deck battery-electric powered BYD DD AD Enviro400EV City double-deckers on the night-time elements of 24-hour routes 43 and 94 respectively during February 2020.'

Route Numbering – Transport for London

When TfL assumed control all routes across the Night Bus network had N-prefixed route numbers. In most instances, route numbers corresponded with daytime services sharing common sections of routeing. A number of routes formed 24-hour services between identical termini, with the night-time element being identified separately by an N-prefix route number.

In the first three years of TfL's control, thirty out of the forty-two new Night Bus route introductions formed 'seamless' 24-hour services with daytime services. LBSL discontinued using N-prefixes to identify the night-time element of almost all 24-hour services between November 2003 and May 2004. Since then those routes, along with almost all 24-hour route introductions since, have used the daytime route number by night as well.

Other Night Bus routes have, in general, continued to be identified with N-prefixed route numbers, the numbers usually indicating affinity with shared common sections of daytime bus routes. Exceptions, at 30/31 December 2020, comprise routes N5 (Trafalgar Square–Edgware), N20 (Trafalgar Square–Barnet), N97 (Trafalgar Square–Hammersmith), N550 (Trafalgar Square–Canning Town) and N551 (Trafalgar Square–Gallions Reach) which have no routeing relationship or numerical affinity with daytime services.

Occasional route numbering anomalies have occurred. Arguably, the most outstanding example happened from 3/4 July 2009 when the night-time element (only) of 24-hour Ealing Broadway to Kingston route 65 was extended a considerable distance beyond Kingston to Chessington but continued to use route number 65, without an N-prefix. The position was regularised from 28/29 September 2018 when the night-time service became N65. Since then, LBSL has become punctilious in identifying night-time variations of 24-hour routes with an N-prefix.

Impact of the Night Tube

TfL announced in 2014 that it planned to introduce Friday and Saturday night operation on certain London Underground lines. The ASLEF, RMT, TSSA and Unite trade unions quickly expressed concerns about pay rates and working conditions, backing this up with a series of strikes affecting daytime Tube services in summer 2015. This caused the Night Tube's planned start date of 11/12 September 2015 to be postponed. Notwithstanding, certain changes to Night Bus routes were implemented from that date. Most significant was the introduction of Friday and Saturday night services over three daytime bus routes which operated from potential Night Tube station hubs at North Greenwich and Morden.

Agreement was reached between the trade unions and London Underground, allowing the first Night Tube services to begin running on 19/20 August 2016. These covered the Central Line, between Ealing Broadway and Loughton or Hainault, and the entire Victoria Line between Walthamstow Central and Brixton. A weekend Night Tube service was instituted over the entire length of the Jubilee Line, between Stanmore and Stratford, from 7/8 October 2016. The third phase of weekend Night Tube operation benefitted the Edgware and High Barnet to Morden via Charing Cross sections of the Northern Line from 18/19 November 2016. The fourth stage of weekend Night Tube service introduction was on 16/17 December 2016 when the Heathrow Terminal 5 to Cockfosters section of the Piccadilly Line gained a service. Fourteen further daytime bus routes gained weekend-nights services from Night Tube hubs.

The introduction of weekend Night Tube services abstracted passengers from the Night Bus network but it took time for reduced demand to work through to allocations. An immediate effect was actually an increased requirement of fifty-two buses to work the seventeen weekend night-time services introduced to serve Night Tube hubs. The Night Bus network reached its highest ever weekend nights peak vehicle requirement (PVR) of 1,049 buses at 11/12 February 2017. The first reductions related to the Night Tube were affected from 1/2 September 2017 when frequency reductions over seven routes caused weekend nights' PVR to be reduced by forty-one buses. The cull continued progressively over the following eight months, after which weekend nights' PVR had been reduced by 19 per cent to 852 buses by 1/2 June 2018.

Coronavirus Pandemic

The coronavirus pandemic has had a profound on TfL's operations. N-prefixed routes and the night-time elements of 24-hour services adopted Sunday to Thursday night schedules on Friday and Saturday nights from 20/21 March 2020. Weekend Night Tube services were suspended from the same night as was operation of the seventeen weekend-only Night Bus services connecting from Night Tube hubs.

Stagecoach East London commenced NHS contracts to provide 24-hour services to the Nightingale Hospital at the Excel Centre from 6 April 2020. Shortly afterwards, routes NG1–4 were absorbed into the TfL system for journey planning purposes with a night-time allocation of nine buses. These routes were short-lived with the final one, NG3, last operating on 13 May 2020. Metroline-operated route N20 was extended beyond Barnet Church to Barnet Hospital from 1/2 April 2020 and continued to terminate there at 30/31 December 2020.

Friday and Saturday night schedules were progressively restored to all N-prefix and the night-time elements of most 24-hour routes during August 2020. Exceptions were the seventeen weekend night services from Night Tube hubs, which, along with the Night Tube, remained suspended at 30/31 December 2020.

Lockdowns, increased home working and official exhortations to avoid using public transport have combined to drastically reduce passenger numbers and revenue across TfL's network. Financial support packages negotiated between the government and Transport for London have kept services running.

Initial Expansion 1984

Trafalgar Square became the convergence point for all central London-serving Night Bus routes. MCW Metrobus M 766 was seen against the imposing backdrop of the National Gallery working a route N90 journey to Hammond Street in Hertfordshire on 29/30 April 1984. (Paul Davis)

Night Buses serving north and east London used bus stop C outside the National Gallery. Wandsworth garage's Leyland Titan T 991 was loading on newly introduced cross-London route N79 (Lewisham–Archway Station). (Paul Davis)

Night Buses to south and west London used bus stop V outside Canada House, on the western perimeter of Trafalgar Square. Peckham garage's Leyland Titan T 844 was working newly introduced route N74 to Bromley North in June 1984. (Paul Davis)

Pre-existing route N82 was revised to form a lengthy cross-London service between Woolwich Arsenal and Kensal Rise. Buses travelling in both directions used bus stop V, as shown by New Cross garage's Leyland Titans T 869, bound for Kensal Rise, and T 863 going to Eltham. (Paul Davis)

Most network expansion from 13/14 April 1984 was achieved by extending existing routes. The only new major route corridor served was along Finchley Road by route N13. From 26/27 October 1984 the N13 was extended to Barnet Church as displayed by Finchley garage's MCW Metrobus M 579 at Trafalgar Square. (Malc McDonald)

Pre-existing route N89 was extended beyond Southall to Uxbridge Station where Hanwell garage's MCW Metrobus M 498 was photographed. (Malc McDonald)

An Emergency Stand-By bus was commissioned from 26/27 October 1984 at Victoria garage to cover missing buses on any central London-serving Night Bus route. GM garage also housed buses used on LRT's daytime sightseeing tour, which were spare at night, and had pressed London Sightseeing Bus M 1045 into service to replace an absent N79 Walworth garage Leyland Titan when seen at Lewisham Bus Station on 8/9 December 1984. (Malc McDonald)

Liverpool Street Station had been a long-established Night Bus terminus since the introduction of the London General Omnibus Company's first all-night bus routes in 1913. *Above*: Stamford Brook garage's MCW Metrobus M 168 was outside adjacent Broad Street Station, site of the current Liverpool Street Bus Station, ready for a short-working journey to Stamford Brook garage over Richmond route N27. *Below*: M 313 was set for an N94 journey to its extended outer terminus at Edgware Station. (Both Paul Davis)

London Regional Transport 1985–99

LRT's development of the Night Bus network sometimes favoured the creation of cross-London services. From 26/27 October 1984 Hampstead Heath route N93 was projected to Hammersmith and further extended to Fulwell garage from 26/27 April 1985. Leyland Titan T 618 was seen at Piccadilly Circus. (Malc McDonald)

Evaluation trials for London's next generation of double-deck buses were held between March 1984 and August 1986 from Stockwell garage. Hestair Dennis Dominators, Leyland Olympians, MCW Metrobuses Mk 2 and Volvo Ailsas were tested and often deployed on route N87. *Above*: Hestair Dennis Dominator H 2 was seen outside Canada House in Trafalgar Square on 14/15 June 1985. *Below*: Leyland won the order, as exemplified by Leyland Olympian L 91 (C91 CHM), seen along Strand in 1987 on a N82 journey. (Both Malc Mcdonald)

Route N68 was projected beyond Wandsworth to Sutton Station from 26/27 April 1985. DMS 2467 was seen at Vauxhall on 1/2 December 1987, not long after the route had been converted to Leyland Fleetline operation from Sutton garage. (Malc McDonald)

Enfield route N 29 underwent multiple frequency increases to become one of London's most successful Night Bus routes. Wood Green garage's MCW Metrobus M 1278 was photographed at Piccadilly Circus on 1/2 December 1987. (Malc McDonald)

LRT acquired fifty Volvo Ailsas from West Midlands Travel in 1987. Potters Bar garage's V 30 was seen in Trafalgar Square with improvised N92 route number displays in its windscreen. (Malc McDonald)

Route N8 was introduced on 12/13 August 1988 as a cross-London service between Bow Church and Queensbury Station. Bow garage's Leyland Titan T 443 was at Tottenham Court Road Station two months later. (Malc McDonald)

Regular service over route N 73 was introduced from 22/23 September 1989. Leaside Buses MCW Metrobus M 1402 was at Victoria Station on that night alongside London Central's Leyland Olympian L 101 (C101 CHM) on route N 72. (Roy Waterhouse)

The first major expansion of the Night Bus network since 13/14 April 1984 took place on 27/28 October 1989 when ten new routes were introduced and others modified or extended. On their inaugural night of operation, *Above*: London Central's Leyland Titan T 991 was on route N3 at Trafalgar Square, *Below*: London Northern's MCW Metrobus M 1082 at Edgware Station working the N5 (note 'Northern Line' branding to emphasise parallel routeing to that Underground line) and *Opposite page above*: London Central's T 687 at Trafalgar Square on route N53. *Opposite page below*: London General's Leyland Fleetline DMS 2287 was loading at Trafalgar Square for a journey to the N87's new terminus at Surbiton Station. (All Roy Waterhouse)

"IT'S THE TOPS"
Elephant New Cross
Lewisham Blackheath
Woolwich Plumstead Com
N53
PLUMSTEAD COMMON
OHV687Y

THE PIRATES OF PENZANCE
Westminster Bdg Oval
Stockwell Clapham
Balham Tooting
N87
SURBITON STATION
THE MIKADO
THX 287S
LONDON GENERAL

Single-deck bus operation returned to the Night Bus network with the introduction of Night Arrow route N31 (Camden Town–Fulham) on 11/12 November 1989. The N31 was soon upgraded to Dennis Darts such as Centrewest's DW 107 (KDZ 5107), in Bayham Street, Camden Town. (Roy Waterhouse)

A host of Night Bus routes had isolated journeys extended in service to/from Victoria so that drivers could use Victoria bus garage's canteen for breaks. Norwood Junction route N69 was one such service, as shown by Leyland Olympian L 196 ready to return from Victoria Station to reach its usual starting point at Trafalgar Square. (Roy Waterhouse)

Some daytime bus routes had isolated early morning journeys into central London. On Mondays to Fridays, between 26 October 1992 and 28 January 1994, route 3B ran unidirectional 04:45, 05:15 and 05:35 journeys from Herne Hill to Holborn Station – despite the destination displayed by Stockwell garage's Northern Counties-bodied Volvo Citybus VC 17 (G117 NGN) in Brixton. (Roy Waterhouse)

London Transport Buses' final batch of Leyland Olympians comprised forty 1992 Alexander RH-bodied models. Leaside Buses' L 323 (J323 BSH) was outside the National Gallery working route N253. (Malc McDonald)

The award of the contract for routes 6/N6 (Aldwych–Kensal Rise) to independent London Suburban Bus, from 28/29 January 1994, was a big surprise. 201 (L201 SKD), in Cockspur Street, was one of ten Volvo Olympians bought for these services. (Malc McDonald)

On 28/29 January 1994 route N159 (Victoria–Edgware Station) was renumbered N139 and revised to operate between Trafalgar Square and West Hampstead. Centrewest's MCW Metrobus M 885 was loading in Cockspur Street shortly afterwards. (Malc McDonald)

The second use of route number N9 occurred from 25/26 February 1994 for a service between Trafalgar Square and Kingston. London United's all-Leyland Olympian L 304 (G 304 UYK) was loading in Piccadilly. (Malc McDonald)

London Central operated a batch of twenty-five DAF DB250/Optare Spectras. SP 9 (K309 FYG) was loading outside Canada House on 4/5 February 1995 for a journey to route N109's bifurcated terminus at Old Coulsdon – alternate N109 journeys ran to New Addington. (Malc McDonald)

London Central's Emergency Stand-By Leyland Titan T 929 had been summoned to replace an absent East London Titan on Walthamstow route N26. Camberwell garage's Stand-By buses were equipped with dot-matrix displays to cover the large number of central London-serving Night Bus routes. (Malc McDonald)

The N31 became the first low-floor Night Bus route, from 1/2 May 1998. First Centrewest's Marshall Capital-bodied Dennis Dart SLF DM 282 was at Notting Hill Gate. (Philip Wallis)

Increasing traffic congestion necessitated re-routeing many Night Bus services away from Trafalgar Square between 1996 and 2000. Amongst such routes, the N68 and N207 were altered to terminate at Tottenham Court Road Station and Holborn respectively, from 28/29 April 2000. *Above*: Earlier, Arriva London South's Leyland Olympian L 63 was loading outside Canada House on 26 June 1999 whilst *Below*: First Centrewest's Northern Counties-bodied Leyland Olympian V 54 was on the south side of Trafalgar Square, with a notice in its windscreen reminding Uxbridge garage's staff that it needed 'TO BE FUELLED' on its return. (Both Philip Wallis)

The last new step-floor double-deckers for London comprised a batch of twenty stock-built Northern Counties Palatine 1-bodied Volvo Olympians delivered to First Centrewest in April 1999. VN 104 was sparkling when photographed on the south side of Trafalgar Square on 26 June 1999, prior to a N18 journey to Harrow Weald. (Philip Wallis)

Two generations of soon-to-be-displaced step-floor double-deckers met at Trafalgar Square on 4 July 1999. London Central's Dulwich-bound N12 Leyland Titan T 977 (right) would have to complete a circuit of the Square to reach bus stop V outside Canada House from where Stagecoach Selkent's Volvo Olympian VN 88 had set off on its N47 journey to Bromley. (Philip Wallis)

Above: First Capital's low-floor Plaxton President-bodied Dennis Trident TN 811 was outside Canada House on 26 June 1999, working Plumstead route N1. *Below*: Stagecoach East London's low-floor Alexander-bodied Dennis Trident TA 77 was in Duncannon Street working a N15 journey to Romford Market on 4 July 1999. (Both Philip Wallis)

Beyond London

Essex and Hertfordshire

Route N18 was extended to Watford Junction (Hertfordshire) on 25/26 September 1987, becoming LRT's longest bus route at 25½ miles. MCW Metrobus M 1426 was loading in Cockspur Street on 1/2 December 1987. The N18 was cut back to terminate at Harrow Weald from 28/29 January 1994. (Malc McDonald)

Route N80 linked North Finchley with Potters Bar garage (Hertfordshire), where MCW Metrobus M 1265 was seen. The N80 last operated on 19/20 June 1986, being replaced by an extension to route N92. (Malc McDonald)

Daytime bus route 279 gained a limited service of four/five night-time journeys to Waltham Cross (Hertfordshire) and Upshire (Essex) from 25/26 September 1987. MCW Metrobus M 733 was in Islington High Street on 15/16 February 1988. The 279's night-time service last operated on 30/31 January 1992. (Malc McDonald)

Route N96 was extended beyond Chingford Station to give a Night Bus service to Loughton and Debden (Essex) from 27/28 October 1989. Stagecoach East London's Leyland Titan T 298 was loading in Trafalgar Square shortly before the N96 was renumbered N38 and its Essex service withdrawn from 14/15 July 1995. (Malc McDonald)

Route N21 became operated by Potters Bar garage from 3/4 December 1993. Nightly positioning journeys ran in service to/from Cockfosters Station but on Friday and Saturday nights an hourly service was maintained between Trafalgar Square and Potters Bar. London Northern's Metrobus M 1390 was in New Oxford Street on Saturday night 4/5 February 1995. (Malc McDonald)

Kent

The N72 was LRT's first Night Bus into Kent when its service to Dartford was introduced from 1/2 November 1985. New Cross garage's Eastern Coach Works-bodied Leyland Olympian L 89 (C89 CHM) was at Camberwell Green on 1/2 December 1987. (Malc McDonald)

Prestigious limited-stop route NX1 to the Medway Towns was usually worked by London Central's coach-seated Leyland Olympian L 261 (2 CLT), loading outside Canada House for the NX1's inaugural journey at 01:00 on Saturday 20 October 1990. (Roy Waterhouse)

London Central's former West Midlands PTE coach-seated Leyland Titan T 1129 (WDA 4T) was another luxury vehicle used on the NX1. (Malc McDonald)

The NX1's service into Kent was absorbed into normal stopping route N81 from 8/9 October 1993. London Central's Leyland Titan T 186 (CUL 186V) was loading outside Canada House for a Gravesend journey on 4/5 February 1995. (Malc McDonald)

London Central's Volvo Olympian NV 85 (R285 LGH) was outside Canada House loading for route N81's sole journey to Gillingham on Sunday morning 4 July 1999, two weeks before LRT-sponsored Night Bus operation into Kent ended. (Philip Wallis)

London Central's Northern Counties-bodied Volvo Olympian NV 79 (R279 LGH) was loading at Trafalgar Square on Sunday morning 8 August 1999 for a Gravesend journey on commercial route N80. Note 'EXPRESS' on the blind. (Philip Wallis)

Surrey

Route N54 operated between East Croydon Station and Banstead (Surrey) between 20/21 June 1986 and 21/22 May 1987. Leyland Fleetline D 2603 was at Sutton Station early on Sunday morning 10 August 1986. (Malc McDonald)

Two journeys on route N88 were projected to/from Banstead from 22/23 May 1987, as was one inbound N68 journey from 31 October/1 November 1987. Leyland Fleetline D 2607 showed an improvised N88 route number display on 1/2 June 1987. Such Banstead journeys last ran on 17/18 August 1995. (Malc McDonald)

Route N67 to Staines was introduced as a Friday and Saturday night service on 5/6 January 1990. MCW Metrobus M 172 was seen in Hounslow one week later. The N67 was later extended to Egham and last operated on 24/25 February 1994. (Roy Waterhouse)

Route N87 was projected beyond Surbiton to Hampton Court Station, on the Surrey bank of the River Thames, from 26/27 April 1991. MCW Metrobus M 279 was loading at Trafalgar Square on 8 June 1991. Hampton Court Station N87 journeys last operated on 17/18 August 1995. (Roy Waterhouse)

Route N97 was revised from 25/26 February 1994 to form a bifurcation at Hounslow, with journeys beyond terminating at either Heathrow Central or Sunbury Village (Surrey). London United's MCW Metrobus M 1345 (C345 BUV) was loading in Piccadilly on 4/5 February 1995. The N97's bifurcation ceased after 29/30 August 1996. (Malc McDonald)

Some Lost LRT Night Routes

Route N91 (Willesden Garage–Liverpool Street) originated in 1913 as the London General Omnibus Company's second all-night bus route 94A. It remained unchanged over subsequent years, apart from one-way traffic systems, and renumbering to 91 in 1924, 291 in 1934 and N91 on 11/12 October 1960. It ran almost parallel to new route N18 and was absorbed into that route from 25/26 October 1984. MCW Metrobus M 218 was at Charing Cross Station. (Paul Davis)

The Inter-Station Route had operated as a night-time-only service since 21/22 November 1950. Leyland Titan T 863 was photographed at Waterloo Station on 21/22 April 1985, its last night of operation. (Paul Davis)

The Inter-Station Route was absorbed into the Night Bus network from 26/27 April 1985 as routes N50 (westbound) and N51 (eastbound) and extended to Ladbroke Grove. Journeys in both directions were numbered N50 from 19/20 June 1986. *Above*: MCW Metrobus M 896 was seen in Shepherds Bush garage on 27 April 1985, ready to work the N50, whilst *Below*: Leyland Titan T 1039 was on the N51 at Russell Square on 19 April 1986. (Paul Davis, Malc McDonald)

A Railair Link service was operated by London Transport under contract to British Rail from 13/14 May 1984. It operated non-stop from Euston Station to Victoria Station (for rail connection to Gatwick Airport) and then non-stop to Heathrow Airport. It later served Waterloo Station additionally. Leyland Titan T 417 was at Euston on 23 June 1984. (Paul Davis)

The Railair Link to Heathrow Airport was incorporated into route N56 from 26/27 April 1985. MCW Metrobus M 1211 was outside Paddington Station on 19 April 1986. The N56 last operated on 20/21 May 1993. (Malc McDonald)

Route N60 was a staff bus service made available for public use whilst Streatham garage was closed for rebuilding work between 26/27 October 1984 and 5/6 February 1987. It followed an unidirectional route between Clapham Common Station and West Croydon, passing four LT garages. MCW Metrobus M 1066 was opposite Streatham garage on 15 June 1985. (Malc McDonald)

Route number N99 has been used three times. The first N99 (Chingford–Victoria & Albert Docks) was introduced on 26/27 April 1960 to replace a former staff trolleybus service. *Above*: Leyland Titan T 436 was at V&A Docks on 17 October 1985, shortly before that N99's withdrawal. The second N99 operated between Romford and Cranham, where *Below*: Leyland Titan T 570 was photographed on 8/9 August 1986, the inaugural night of operation. There was a hiatus in operation during early 1987 until a unidirectional N99 was restored between Romford (later Chadwell Heath) and Cranham from 27/28 March 1987, operated by Ensignbus. *Opposite page above*: Leyland Fleetline B 217 (KJD 500P), former LT DMS 2000, was at Romford Market on 23/24 May 1987. This version of the N99 last operated on 7/8 September 1991. The third N99 started on 17/18 July 1992 for a new service between Trafalgar Square and Queensbury Station. *Opposite page below*: MCW Metrobus M 1346 was in Willesden High Street on 26 July 1992. This third N99 was renumbered N98 on 18/19 August 1995. (Malc McDonald, Paul Davis, Malc McDonald, Roy Waterhouse)

Ensignbus
N99
CRANHAM

METROLINE
N99
TRAFALGAR SQUARE
C346BUV
BUS STOP
DRUG STORE
KEEP BRENT

Special New Year's Eve shuttle bus services operated across central London on New Year's Eves between 1989 and 2004, as well as 2006. *Above*: London United's MCW Metrobus M 295 was in Aldwych operating a non-stop shuttle to Victoria on 1 January 1990. *Below*: Between New Year's Eves 1993 and 1999 the shuttle was numbered N100, as shown by London Northern's Metrobus M 921 in Aldwych on 1 January 1993. (Both Roy Waterhouse)

The first N9 was introduced on 9/10 February 1990. It operated occasional journeys between Enfield Town and central London via Southgate as well as an isolated 05:00 journey from Palmers Green to Turnpike Lane Station via Edmonton. Leaside Buses MCW Metrobus M 605 was loading at Victoria Station on 17 February 1990. This N9 last operated on 24/25 June 1993. (Roy Waterhouse)

The N66 operated one unidirectional journey at 02:20 on Friday, Saturday and Sunday nights from Cricklewood to Edgware Station via Willesden, Harlesden and Wembley. Despite an excellent blind display and large route board in its windscreen, Metroline's MCW Metrobus M 1198 was empty at Cricklewood Broadway on 31 October 1992, inaugural night of operation. The N66 last ran on 23/24 January 1994. (Roy Waterhouse)

Route N70 had varied routeings following its introduction on 27/28 October 1989. Latterly, it operated between Trafalgar Square and Norwood Junction and was LRT's last Friday and Saturday night-only Night Bus. London Central's Volvo Olympian AV1 was outside Canada House on 26 June 1999 on a short-working to New Cross Gate. The N70 was incorporated into nightly route N381 from 8/9 October 1999. (Philip Wallis)

Transport for London from 2000

(All pictures by Philip Wallis)

Typifying new low-floor buses which flooded into service from 2000 onwards are *Above*: Arriva London North's DAF DB250LF DLA 277, sweeping into Trafalgar Square from Whitehall on route N24, and *Below*: Metroline's Volvo B7TL VPL 135 on the N43, waiting departure from bus stop C outside the National Gallery.

MCW Metrobus operation on Night Bus routes ended during October 2001. Metroline's M 306 was setting off from Victoria Bus Station for its N16 journey to Edgware Station on Wednesday morning 13 July 2001.

London General's Volvo Olympian NV 139 (R339 LGH) was photographed at Putney Bridge Station working the inaugural route N93 journey to North Cheam at 0130 on Saturday morning 1 December 2001. The N93 was the last Night Bus route to be introduced using step-floor buses.

Relief breaks for many Night Bus drivers were taken in Victoria garage's canteen, with buses making special in-service journeys to/from Victoria. Following closure of that garage in 1993, a mobile canteen was provided at Victoria Bus Station; latterly *Right top:* London Central's Leyland Titan T 875 fulfilled that role. A change in policy scheduling relief breaks away from central London ended this practice after 27/28 June 2002. *Right middle:* London Central's Volvo B7TL PVL 215, returning from Victoria to the N81's usual terminus at Trafalgar Square, was at the top of Whitehall alongside Routemaster RML 2396, first bus of the day on route 12.

Cross-London route N19 (Finsbury Park Station–Clapham Junction) was in the process of conversion to low-floor operation when Arriva London South's step-floor Leyland Olympian L 239 was seen at Hyde Park Corner on 5 July 2002.

Routeing and stops for Night Buses at Trafalgar Square changed profoundly from 1 September 2002. The northern carriageway, being used by *Above*: Sovereign London's DAF DB250LF 30, was closed to vehicular traffic and pedestrianised. Two-way traffic flows were introduced on other sides of the Square, resulting in the loss of the parking area for layover buses on the south side, where *Below*: Arriva London North's DAF DLA 269 was seen. Two-way traffic flow was restored to Cockspur Street for the first time since 1926, shown by *Opposite page above*: Connex Bus's Dennis Trident TA 28 heading south in 2003. *Opposite page below*: LBSL had provided an information van at Trafalgar Square for Night Bus users, such as Ford Transit X188 CBH, but that practice ceased after the road changes.

N3
OXFORD CIRCUS
Top of the mornings.
connex
Y328 KGW

Bus information
X188 GBH

Route N189 (Oxford Circus–North Cricklewood, later Brent Cross) began on 11/12 October 2002. Metroline's TransBus Trident TP 402 was at Baker Street Station.

Route N63 (King's Cross–Crystal Palace) started from 15/16 November 2002. London Central's Volvo B7TL AVL 26 waited at the southern side of Blackfriars Bridge, near the spot where some of London's earliest all-night horse-tram services had terminated in 1899.

Roehampton route N74 was introduced on 22/23 November 2002. London General's Volvo B7TL WVL 47 was at that route's inbound Baker Street Station terminus in Marylebone Road.

The N453 (Marylebone Station–Deptford) was the first Night Bus route to be operated by bendy buses, from March 2003. Stagecoach Selkent's articulated Mercedes-Benz Citaro 23001 was at Baker Street Station stop in Marylebone Road.

Volume delivery of new low-floor buses meant that only six Night Bus routes had full or partial step-floor bus allocations at the beginning of 2003. Arriva London North's step-floor Leyland Olympian L 324 was seen departing from Victoria Bus Station before route N38 became low-floor in April 2003.

First London's step-floor Dennis Arrow 442 passed Nelson's Column as it left Trafalgar Square, bound for Barnet on 5 June 2003. The LBSL contract for route N20 was reassigned to Metroline from 25/26 July 2003.

Route N7 (Russell Square–Northolt Station) was introduced on 29/30 August 2003. First London's Volvo B7TL VTL 1228 was starting its inbound journey from Northolt Station.

Highgate Village route N214 was operated by step-floor Dennis Darts upon its introduction from 1/2 September 2000 and converted to low-floor bus operation in summer 2003. Metroline's Dennis Dart SLF DLS 3 was at Liverpool Street Bus Station on 1 November 2003.

The LBSL contract for route N50 was transferred from First London to Stagecoach East London on 29/30 August 2003. Dennis Trident 17169 was at East Beckton District Centre on 25 April 2004.

Night-time elements of almost all 24-hour services lost their distinguishing 'N' route number prefixes between November 2003 and May 2004. *Above*: First London's Volvo B7TL VNW 32384 displayed plain route number 27 during its night-time journey along Marylebone Road. *Below*: Metrobus' Scania OmniDekka 496 showed plain route number 119 at East Croydon Station. *Opposite page above*: An anomaly was created with route 250 since its night-time element followed a different routeing to its daytime service to serve East Croydon Station at night only, as shown by Arriva London South's VDL DW 58 at that location. This was only regularised from 1/2 November 2019 with renumbering of the night-time service to N250. *Opposite page below*: Some drivers resented loss of the N-prefix and continued to display it as long as possible. East Thames Buses' Volvo Merit DWL 34 displayed N108 at Lewisham Station as late as 24 March 2006 – extraordinary considering that East Thames was a subsidiary of LBSL, which determined route numbering policy.

250
Brixton Station
ARRIVA
LJ04 LFD
E6

Lewisham
CGL
Stratford Stn N108
Lewisham

London's final two bifurcated Night Bus routes last operated on 24/25 June 2004. *Above* and *below*: Stagecoach East London's TransBus Tridents 17757 and 18212 were at route N8's alternative outer termini at Woodford Wells and Newbury Park Station respectively. *Opposite page above*: On 6 June 2004, First London's Dennis Trident TN 1041 was leaving Romford Station for route N25's terminus at Harold Hill *Opposite page below*: whilst TN 1066 was approaching the N25's other terminus in Hainault.

Stratford St Paul's Aldgate Holborn N25
Harold Hill
L'ORÉAL
PARIS
First London
First
TN1041
LN51 DWF

Stratford St Paul's Aldgate Holborn N25
Hainault The Lowe
GAP
First London
First
LN51 GLF

Route 25 became a bendy bus-operated 24-hour service between Oxford Circus and Ilford from 25/26 June 2004. Running number WA 101 indicated that Stagecoach East London's articulated Mercedes-Benz Citaro 23073 had been allocated to the 25's night-time service when photographed in New Oxford Street.

Route N155 ran parallel to the Morden section of the Underground's Northern Line with a 15-minute weeknight and 10-minute weekend nights frequency when London General's Volvo B7TL EVL 6 was seen at Charing Cross Station on 18 July 2004.

Routes N28 and N31 shared a lengthy common section of routeing between Camden Town and Kensington High Street before splitting to their southern termini at Wandsworth and Clapham Junction respectively. The pair remained the last LBSL routes with hourly frequencies on weeknights until increased to 30 minutes from 29/30 April 2016. *Above and below*: First London's Volvo B7TL VNW 32390 and TransBus Trident TNA 33364 were at Notting Hill Gate on 28 August 2004.

The N381 was the last Night Bus route with a step-floor bus allocation. London General's Volvo Olympian NV 52 was at Peckham Bus Station on Sunday morning 18 July 2004, three months before the N381's LBSL contract was reassigned to Travel London using low-floor Volvos.

Arriva London North's DAF DB250LF DLA 198 was Victoria-bound at the Waltham Cross terminus of route N279 on 19 September 2004, shortly before that route's central London terminus was cut back to Trafalgar Square from 15/16 October 2004.

On New Year's Eve 2005 forty-one daytime bus routes were given night-time services for that night only, a practice which has been perpetuated since, although routes have varied. First London's Dennis Trident TN 33062 was photographed at 03:02 on 1 January 2005 at Turnpike Lane Station when working Wood Green to Ilford route 123.

Route N5 runs parallel to the Northern Line's Edgware branch and was a high-demand service before Night Tubes started in 2016. Metroline's Volvo B7TL VPL 225 was at Tottenham Court Road Station on 19 February 2005.

The contract for Thamesmead route N1 had recently been awarded to LBSL's subsidiary East Thames Buses when Volvo B7TL VP 8 was loading in Kingsway on 6 December 2005.

Busy Enfield Town route N29 was converted to bendy bus operation on 13/14 January 2006, requiring an allocation of fifteen articulated Mercedes-Benz Citaros on weeknights and twenty-four at weekends. Arriva London North's MA 130 was at Tottenham Court Road Station on 11 June 2006.

Stagecoach sold its London bus operations to Australian Macquarie Bank on 30 August 2006. East London's TransBus Trident 18206 was in Wilton Road, Victoria, starting point for its lengthy N8 journey to Hainault. After sustaining operating losses, Macquarie sold the businesses back to Stagecoach on 14 October 2010.

Sutton route N44 was substantially re-routed from 10/11 November 2006 to travel via Victoria and Chelsea Bridge rather than Westminster Bridge and Vauxhall. London General's Volvo B7TL WVL 131 was in Buckingham Palace Road near Victoria Station.

Ten daytime bus routes gained night-time operations to become 24-hour services in 2007. One such was Ladbroke Grove to Clapham Junction route 295. First London's Volvo B7TL VNW 32374 was in Falcon Road on 30 September 2007.

Go-Ahead Docklands Buses' route 474 (Canning Town–Manor Park) became a 24-hour service from 2/3 November 2007. There was much interchange of vehicles with Go-Ahead Blue Triangle, shown by the latter's Scania OmniDekka SO 4 in High Street, Manor Park, on 29 June 2008.

Route N551 was introduced on 29/30 August 2008 when it partially replaced the N50. Go-Ahead Docklands Buses' Scania OmniCity SOC 2 was at Canning Town Bus Station on 14 September 2008.

Travel London's bus operation was sold to Dutch Ned Railways on 9 June 2009, which rebranded the operation as Abellio. Before the sale, *Above*: Travel London's Volvo B7TL 9069 was in Waterloo Road in April 2009, working a night-time journey to North Greenwich on 24-hour route 188. *Below*: Post-sale, similar Volvo 9017, on Peckham route N381, displayed Abellio branding in York Road, Waterloo.

Alexander-Dennis Trident Enviro400s gained a substantial share of London's double-deck bus market. *Above*: Metroline's TE 881 was at Waterloo Way working a night-time journey on 24-hour route 139 in April 2009. *Below*: Arriva London South's T 120, painted 100 per cent red as stipulated by TfL, was on London Bridge in October 2010, working Liverpool Street to Mitcham route N133.

Romford Market to Paddington Basin route N15 was at its longest extent when East London's TransBus Trident 17879 was photographed at Romford Station on 20 July 2010. One month later, the N15's central London terminus was cut back to Regent Street.

Arriva London North's articulated Mercedes-Benz Citaro MA 60 was at the 149's London Bridge terminus on 4 April 2009. 24-hour route 149 was converted from bendy bus to double-deck operation on 15/16 October 2010.

Crossrail construction works caused much disruption to bus routes. A long diversion, between February 2011 and May 2012, affected eastbound bus routes using Oxford Street. First London's TransBus Trident TN 33193 was some distance from the N207's normal line of route when photographed along Marylebone Road on 10 December 2011.

FirstGroup sold the bulk of its London bus operations on 22 June 2013. 24-hour route 23 was amongst services acquired by Tower Transit. The new owner had not delayed applying its modest logo to the front of hybrid AD Enviro400H DNH 39131 when seen at Charing Cross Station on 10 July 2013.

Route 205 was the first post-2004 24-hour service to gain an N-prefix when its night-time service (only) was extended beyond Bow to Leyton from 30/31 August 2013. Stagecoach East London's Scania OmniCity 15121 was at Euston Station on 21 September 2013.

The N38 was the first N-prefixed Night Bus route to gain New Routemaster operation, from 15/16 May 2014. Arriva London North's LT 207 was in New Oxford Street on 5 August 2014.

Cross-London Night Bus routes are few nowadays but the N19 has maintained that status since the introduction of its Clapham Junction to Finsbury Park Station service on 27/28 October 1989. Twenty-five years later Go-Ahead London General's hybrid Volvo B5LH WHV 19 was in New Oxford Street on 5 August 2014.

Walthamstow Central route N73 was in transition to New Routemaster operation when Arriva London North's LT 499 was seen at Victoria Station on 17 June 2015. The N73 was truncated to terminate at Oxford Circus exactly two years later.

Some Lost TfL Night Routes

(All pictures by Philip Wallis)

Wanstead to North Woolwich route N101 started on 27/28 April 2001 but only survived until 16/17 September 2004. Stagecoach East London's TransBus Trident 17849 was at East Beckton District Centre on 25 April 2004.

The N58 was another short-lived east London route. In accordance with policy, this 24-hour service lost its N-prefix from 26/27 March 2004. Stagecoach East London's TransBus Trident 18243 was at Walthamstow Central Bus Station in the early hours of 19 February 2005, two weeks before withdrawal of the 58's night service.

Lewisham to Croydon route N75 was introduced on 8/9 February 2002. Stagecoach Selkent's Dennis Trident 17479s was photographed on layover at the former bus station in Lewisham on 5 July 2003. This 24-hour service was numbered 75 from 19/20 March 2004 but its night-time element last operated on 17/18 May 2007.

Regular service over route N36, which varied from the daytime 36 by serving Trafalgar Square, was introduced on 8/9 October 1993. The N36 was replaced by 24-hour route 36 and new route N136 from 8/9 February 2008. London Central's Volvo B7TL PVL 336 was in Terminus Place at Victoria Station on 4 October 2003.

Finsbury Park Station to Aldgate route N106 existed between 27/28 April 2001 and 24/25 April 2008. Stagecoach East London's Dennis Trident 17522s was at Finsbury Park Station on 29 January 2005.

Route N213 (Kingston–Sutton) was introduced on 28/29 June 2002 and extended to West Croydon between 12/13 December 2003 and 2/3 July 2009. It then reverted to 24-hour operation between Kingston and Sutton as 213. London General's Volvo B7TL EVL 4 was in Park Street, Croydon, on 26 June 2005.

Route N274 (Lancaster Gate–Islington) started on 31 January/1 February 2003, losing its N-route number prefix from 19/20 March 2004. Metroline's Dennis Dart SLF DLD 176 was in Bayham Street, Camden Town, on 16 August 2009 with night-time running number HT 861. The 274's night-time service last operated on 23/24 June 2011.

Finsbury Park Station to Hackney Wick route N236 started on 29/30 September 2000 and lost its N-route number prefix from 16/17 April 2004. First London's Marshall Capital-bodied Dennis Dart SLF DM 41734 was leaving Finsbury Park Station on 29 January 2005. Night-time service on the 236 ceased from 5/6 October 2012.

Route N35 (Trafalgar Square–Clapham Junction) began on 25/26 April 1997, terminating at Tottenham Court Road Station from 28/29 April 2000. The N35 was incorporated into 24-hour Shoreditch–Clapham Junction route 35 from 29/30 April 2016. Travel London's AD Trident Enviro400 9460 was in New Oxford Street on 28 June 2009.

Route N64 (Thornton Heath–New Addington) was introduced from 27/28 August 2010, complementing the daytime 64 but with different routeing in New Addington. Metrobus' Scania OmniCity 966 was in London Road, West Croydon, on 30 March 2012. The N64 was aligned and incorporated into 24-hour route 64 from 26/27 August 2016.

Route N13 originated on 13/14 April 1984 and operated between Aldwych and North Finchley from 31 August/1 September 2001. In a complex range of route changes affecting Finchley Road services from 31 March/1 April 2017, the N13 was withdrawn, its night-time service being partially incorporated into 24-hour routes 13 and 139. Transdev London Sovereign's Scania OmniDekka SLE 38 had paused in Finchley Road, Golders Green, on 16 August 2009.

The N10 originated as lengthy cross-London Archway Station to Richmond route on 28/29 September 2001. Its northern terminus was cut back to King's Cross Station from 3/4 September 2004. *Right top:* First London's TransBus Trident TNA 33353 was in New Oxford Street on 28 June 2009. *Right middle:* The N10's service was incorporated into 24-hour route 10 (King's Cross Station–Hammersmith) from 29/30 January 2010. London United's Scania OmniCity SP 163 was at Euston Station on 10 December 2011. The 10 last operated on 21/22 November 2018, being partially incorporated into 24-hour route 23.

Night-time operation was added to route C2 (Parliament Hill Fields–Oxford Circus) from 13/14 April 2007. It was projected via Berkeley Square to Victoria from 26/27 June 2009 (replaced N8) but withdrawn over that section from 14/15 July 2017 (replaced by N22). 24-hour C2 was withdrawn after 29 March 2019. Metroline's Volvo B7TL VP 504 was at Victoria Station on 27 September 2009.

Night Buses 2019

(All pictures by Philip Wallis)

24-hour route 214 was converted to operation by BYD-AD Enviro200EV battery-electric buses from 16/17 August 2019 when its night-time service became the first to be operated by electrically powered vehicles since night trolleybus services ended in 1961. London General's SEe 91 was at Finsbury Square, Moorgate.

Hackney Community Transport's first Night Bus operation was Chingford route N26, from 26/27 February 2016. Trading as CT Plus, AD Enviro 400H 2537 was at Charing Cross Station on 7 June 2019.

Hounslow to Richmond route H37 is representative of routes which gained a weekends-only night-time service with the introduction of Night Tubes. RATP-DEV London United's AD Enviro200 (MMC) DXE 30352 was in London Road, Hounslow, on 21 December 2019.

Route N137 is unusual in that it uses a different bus type to the LT-type New Routemasters allocated to complementary daytime route 137. Arriva London South's Volvo B5LH HV 388 was in Oxford Street loading for Crystal Palace.

New Routemasters operate on twenty-two Night Bus services. *Above*: Route N55 gained New Routemasters in January 2015. Stagecoach East London's LT 314 was loading in New Oxford Street. *Below*: 24-hour route 12 was converted in January 2015. LT 452 had set down north of Oxford Circus in Regent Street. Overall advertising has become a striking feature on New Routemasters. *Opposite page above*: Abellio-operated route N3 became New Routemaster-operated in February 2016. LT 696 was in Cockspur Street followed by another Abellio LT on 24-hour route 159. *Opposite page below*: Go-Ahead Blue Triangle uses New Routemasters on east London routes EL1, EL2 and EL3. Some are spare at night and form part of Romford route N15's allocation. LT 925 displayed East London Transit branding at Charing Cross Station on 21 December 2019.

Bromley North N3
abellio
LT696
STARLING BANK
Mixing pleasure with business.
N3 Bromley North
LTZ 1696
159

Oxford Circus N15
East London Transit
LT925
LTZ 2125

Between June 2018 and December 2019, the night-time elements of twelve 24-hour services gained N-prefixed route numbers, mostly due to shortening of their complementary daytime services. *Above*: Route number N25 was reinstated from 30 November/1 December 2018 when the daytime 25 was curtailed at Holborn Circus. Tower Transit's Wright StreetDeck WH 31109 headed a line of N25 buses at its Oxford Circus terminus in Holles Street. *Below*: Use of route number N33 occurred from 17/18 May 2019 when the daytime 33 was curtailed south of closed Hammersmith Bridge but a night-time service was maintained between Hammersmith and Fulwell by the N33 travelling across Putney Bridge. RATP London United's AD Enviro200 DE 20127 was at Hammersmith's Lower Bus Station. *Opposite page above*: Route number N140 came back into use from 6/7 December 2019 when the daytime 140 from Harrow Weald was curtailed at Hayes & Harlington Station. Metroline's Volvo B5LH VWH 2217 loaded at Heathrow Central Bus Station. *Opposite page below*: Route number N266 was revived when the daytime 266 was truncated to terminate at Acton from 6/7 December 2019. RATP London United's AD Enviro400 ADE 40441 was at Hammersmith's Lower Bus Station.

Harrow Weald
BUS GARAGE
N140
Metroline
LK16 HZJ

Brent Cross
LONDON UNITED
RATP GROUP

Just two new N-prefixed Night Bus routes have been introduced since 2010, excluding the renumbering of night-time elements of 24-hour services. *Above*: Route N113 began on 29/30 June 2012 when it provided an alternative service between Edgware Station and Trafalgar Square via Mill Hill and Brent Cross. Metroline's MCV-bodied Volvo B5LH VMH 2531 was in Oxford Street. *Below*: Route N199 started on 11/12 September 2015 when it replaced much of the N47's outer section to St Mary Cray as well as giving a new link to Greenwich. Stagecoach Selkent's AD Enviro400H-bodied Volvo B5LH 13090 had arrived at Charing Cross Station.